CENGAGE Learning

Drama for Students, Volume 23

Project Editor: Sara Constantakis

Editorial: Anne Marie Hacht, Ira Mark Milne **Rights Acquisition and Management**: Lisa Kincade, Timothy Sisler **Manufacturing**: Drew Kalasky

Imaging: Lezlie Light, Mike Logusz, Kelly A. Quin **Product Design**: Pamela A. E. Galbreath

Product Manager: Meggin Condino

of the publisher and verified to the satisfaction of the publisher will be corrected in future editions.

ISBN 0-7876-8119-9
ISSN 1094-9232

Printed in the United States of America
10 9 8 7 6 5 4 3 2 1

Accidental Death of an Anarchist

Dario Fo

1970

Introduction

Dario Fo's *Accidental Death of an Anarchist* (1970) responds to events unfolding in Italy in the late 1960s and early 1970s. Generally, it looks at police corruption and suspicions regarding the government's collusion in this corruption. More specifically, it addresses the actual death of an anarchist who was being held in police custody following the bombing of a Milan bank that killed sixteen people and wounded about ninety. The police asserted that the anarchist's death was a suicide, that the man threw himself from a fourth-floor window in despair at being found out for his crime. At the subsequent inquest, the presiding judge declared the death not a suicide but an accident. Most Italians believed that the death was the result of overly harsh interrogation techniques, if not a case of outright murder on the part of the interrogators.

Accidental Death of an Anarchist is mainly about police corruption, underscored by the play's focus on impersonation, infiltration, and double-talk. A fast-talking major character, the Maniac, infiltrates a police headquarters. Posing as an investigating judge, he tricks the policemen into contradicting themselves and admitting that they are part of a cover-up involving the death of an anarchist. In infiltrating police headquarters by misrepresenting himself (impersonation), the Maniac reminds audiences of how most political groups in Italy, particularly left-wing groups, were infiltrated by police agents who acted as informers. The Maniac's flip-flop of point of view and statement achieves much the same effect as his impersonations do. His confusing speechifying leads to the police contradicting themselves, so that the Maniac, in all of his deceptions and distortions, is a precise reflection of what the play is designed to expose.

Accidental Death of an Anarchist is one of Fo's

most popular plays both within and outside Italy. It has played around the world over the years to millions of people, a popular choice of directors who want to point to corruption in their midst. Pluto Press (London) put out the first English version, translated by Gavin Richards. In 1992, Methuen published a fine set of volumes of Fo's plays, which included *Accidental Death of an Anarchist*.

Author Biography

Dario Fo is one of Italy's most important and well-known literary figures, along with his partner and longtime collaborator, Franca Rame. He was born in San Giano, Italy, on March 24, 1926, the son of Felice (a railroad stationmaster) and Pina (Rota) Fo. Initially, Fo considered a career in architecture, but before he had quite finished this course of study, he discovered that he was far happier working in theatrical circles. By 1950, Fo had decided definitely on a career on the stage and began to compose plays prolifically. In June of 1954, Fo and Rame married; they have three children.

Running throughout Fo's career are certain constants. His plays are usually farcical with a satirical bite, and they tend to employ popular elements, such as slapstick. This said, there are also discernible stages in Fo's career. At first, he concentrated on creating comical farces and revues, some of which were broadcast on radio. Then, Fo's plays began to resemble more typical dramas, at least in the sense that they became less episodic and less strictly comical in effect. Later, Fo's greater engagement with Italian politics in his plays became evident. Indeed, by the time of *Morte accidentale di un anarchico (Accidental Death of an Anarchist)*, Fo was so deep into Italian politics that he began gearing his plays toward working-class audiences instead of more typical theatergoers. He continued to attract people of all social strata to his plays, yet he began to reflect, theatrically, his sense that his life as an artist is best led in the service of those holding the least amount of social and political power in Italian society. *Accidental Death of an Anarchist* was first produced in Milan in December of 1970; it was staged on Broadway at the Belasco Theater in November 1984.

Fo is a highly influential figure in theatrical circles in and outside Italy. He has written hundreds of pieces across genres (songs, screenplays, plays) and media (stage, radio, film). His plays, which number more than forty, include *I sani da legare* ("A Madhouse for the Sane," 1954), which characterizes certain government officials as fascist sympathizers, and *Mistero buffo* (1969), a controversial improvisational play, based on the Gospels, that disparages both church and state. *L'Anomal bicefalo* ("Two-Headed Anomaly"), produced in Milan in 2003 but not published or translated into English, is a scathing satire of Italy's prime minister, Silvio Berlusconi. Fo has always been an actor in his own work; indeed, he is as well known an actor as he is a writer. He is as beloved and respected by some as he is detested and feared by others, such as those who disagree with him politically. He has even been arrested and put on trial for subversion, and he has been beaten up by rogue political foes, a fate also suffered by his collaborator, Franca Rame. Fo is, in short, a presence to contend with, an artist whose influence and genius are reflected in his having been awarded the Nobel Prize in Literature in 1997.

Act 1, Scene 1

Accidental Death of an Anarchist opens in a room in a police station, where Inspector Bertozzo is interviewing the Maniac, reviewing his arrest record. He notes that the Maniac has been arrested many times for impersonation, the same reason for his arrest this time. The Maniac points out that although he has been arrested, he has never been convicted of a crime. He tells the inspector that he is insane, that he cannot be charged because he is mad. The inspector, incredulous, continues posing questions to the Maniac. The Maniac evades the inspector's questions and denies any real wrongdoing. For example, in response to the inspector's accusation that the Maniac has not only been impersonating a psychiatrist but also actually seeing patients and charging them substantial sums, the Maniac points out that all psychiatrists charge too much. The inspector replies that the specific charges are not the real issue; rather it is the question of impersonation. He points to a visiting card the Maniac has been distributing, which states that the Maniac is a psychiatrist. The Maniac quibbles over a point of punctuation, telling the inspector that, given the placement of a particular comma on the card, he cannot be said to be misrepresenting himself at all. Utterly frustrated, Inspector Bertozzo tells the Maniac that he can go.

The Maniac leaves the room, as does the inspector, for the latter is late to a meeting. The Maniac then pokes his head back into the room and, seeing that it is empty, enters and begins rifling through papers he sees on the inspector's desk. They are arrest sheets. He destroys whatever arrest sheets he feels deserve to be destroyed, leaving intact those he believes describe truly heinous crimes.

Next, the Maniac moves to the inspector's file cabinets. He is about to set fire to the whole lot of them, when he notices a dossier whose name he begins to read out loud, as follows: "Judge's Report on the Death of the ..."; "Judge's Decision to Adjourn the Inquest of...." The Maniac's words would alert the audience to the play's major topic, the death of a suspected anarchist whom most persons in Italy believed was innocent of the crimes for which he was being interrogated when he fell to his death from a window at a police headquarters. The phone rings, and the Maniac answers. It is another police inspector, calling from the fourth floor. The Maniac's words make it clear that the audience is to recall the inspector who conducted the interview with the (real) anarchist who fell or was pushed from a fourth-floor window.

The Maniac's words also make it clear that this second inspector wishes to speak to Bertozzo because he has heard that a judge is coming to the station to ask questions about the anarchist's death. The Maniac pretends that Bertozzo is in the room and making rude comments about the fourth-floor inspector. He tells the inspector that Bertozzo is saying that he might as well accept the fact that his career is over. From the Maniac's side of the conversation, it is clear that the inspector is becoming incensed, highly insulted by what he believes is Inspector Bertozzo's rude and flippant reaction to his concerns. When the Maniac hangs up, it occurs to him that he might impersonate the expected judge. He begins to practice characterizations of a judge.

At this point, Bertozzo reenters the room. He tells the Maniac to get out of the station and is surprised when the Maniac informs him that someone is looking for him to punch him in the face. Sure enough, the fourth-floor inspector arrives outside Bertozzo's door, and the audience sees an arm stretch out to punch Bertozzo in the face.

Act 1, Scene 2

The Maniac, a Constable, and the fourth-floor inspector, who is referred to as Sports Jacket, are in a room at the police station. The Maniac's behavior is mercurial. At one moment, he questions the inspector and Constable severely, as if he knows they are somehow responsible for the anarchist's death. This makes them very nervous. At other moments, however, he appears to be on their side, suggesting that while they might not have told the entire truth about the event, they are right to present themselves as innocent of any wrongdoing. Although they are somewhat befuddled, the two police officers trust in the judge's good intentions.

Then the Maniac, still acting as a judge, asks for the Superintendent to be called into the room. The Superintendent arrives, angry at the peremptory way in which he was summoned. Once he sees that a judge is present, he calms down. The Maniac begins questioning the Superintendent. He asks him to review the item of evidence that says that the anarchist fell from the window because he was seized by a raptus, a state of suicidal anxiety pursuant to extreme desperation. Sports Jacket and the Superintendent begin explaining the events that took place immediately before the anarchist's death, saying that while their line of interrogation and methods might have caused the anarchist's raptus, these methods had not been unreasonable. As the Maniac continues questioning the men, they begin to contradict themselves on many details, such as the precise time of the anarchist's raptus. The Maniac is finally able to declare that the men lied to the media, their superiors, and the original inquest judge. Completely flustered, the two men become even more helpless in the face of the Maniac's mad patter and questions. The act ends with the two policemen completely perplexed, singing an anarchist song in concert with the Maniac.

Act 2, Scene 1

The action begins with the same assembled characters. The Maniac is questioning the policemen about the anarchist's fall from the window. Was the anarchist leaning out for air? Considering the weather, why was the window open at all? Once again, there are discrepancies in what the policemen said at the inquest—that is, what is on record—and what they say to the Maniac. The Maniac is able to get them to begin changing their stories and contradicting themselves. Throughout, real facts and statements from the historical inquest and actual newspaper interviews are used.

A journalist, Maria Feletti, arrives at the station to interview the Superintendent about the anarchist's death. The policemen want to send her away, but the Maniac encourages them to allow her to ask questions. The men say that the Maniac must then leave, as his presence will only give her confidence; she must not know that a judge is interested in questioning them, too. The Maniac persuades them to let him stay, saying that he will impersonate a forensics expert. He wants to stay, he says, to help them manage the Journalist's questions. The Journalist's questions, like those of the Maniac, are peppered with facts and reports from the actual historical inquest and the real interviews with the Milan officials involved in the case. She focuses on discrepancies in the policemen's stories. First, she asks about the nature of the anarchist's fall. There were no broken bones in the body, she says. One expects broken arms and hands in a person who has fallen from a window, because the person would try to break his or her fall. The lack of broken bones suggests that the anarchist was already dead before he fell. The Maniac agrees with her, to the consternation of the assembled policemen.

Next, the Journalist asks the policemen about

the mark that was discovered on the anarchist's neck. It was not consistent with the fall. Is this evidence of a blow to the back of the neck that killed the anarchist? She believes this might be so, because an ambulance had been called for the anarchist before he is said to have fallen. Was the ambulance summoned because he had been given a terrible blow? If he died from the punch, perhaps he was then thrown out the window to make his death look like an accident, she conjectures. At this point, the Maniac begins speaking of the flimsiness of the anarchist's alibi, as if to aid the policemen, yet his intention is instead to discourse on the plight of the working class. According to the Maniac, the anarchist's friends, who vouched for his presence at the time of the bombing, could not possibly remember accurately because they are old, used up from too much work, even malnourished and senile.

Bertozzo enters the room. He has with him a copy of the bomb that was set off in the bank in question. When Bertozzo catches sight of the Maniac, he is about to blurt out that the Maniac is not who he says he is, but the Superintendent and Sports Jacket prevent him from speaking. They believe he is going to say that the Maniac is a judge, which would be disastrous, given what they have told the Journalist. In fact, all Bertozzo knows is that the Maniac cannot be the forensics expert he is claiming to be, because Bertozzo is acquainted with the expert.

The Journalist begins talking about the bomb. Why was a second bomb found at the site of the bombing destroyed? Why was it not saved as evidence? If it had been saved, they would have a "signature" of the bombers, she says. This suggests a cover-up on the part of the police. As she puts it, the anarchist and his group were a ragtag band of dreamers, incapable of planning any such event and certainly not equipped to make such sophisticated bombs. Bertozzo, to the dismay of the Superintendent, agrees. He says that the bomb most likely was made by paramilitary professionals. This idea leads the Journalist to present a common theory, namely, that the bombing was organized by fascists with police support, in order to discredit left-wing organizations and frighten the people into voting for the type of government that is highly supportive of police controls. The idea is that a frightened populace submits to strong, controlling leadership, willingly giving up freedoms in return for perceived safety. As before, the Maniac pretends to be helping the policemen but instead leads them to contradict themselves.

The play ends both comically and seriously. Comically, the Maniac runs through a number of impersonations in the last moments of the play. Less comically, the Maniac speaks of scandal. He says that scandal does not necessarily bring about justice, that it does not inevitably end the careers of those involved in it. Rather, he says, it provides a brief outlet for public anger that then dissipates quickly, so that the status quo is reestablished. The play ends with the Maniac's announcement that he has recorded everything that has transpired and will send copies of his recordings to all media outlets and higher authorities.

Characters

Inspector Bertozzo

Of the three upper-echelon police characters appearing in *Accidental Death of an Anarchist*, Inspector Bertozzo spends the least amount of time on stage. He has a role at the play's beginning, as the policeman interviewing the Maniac for impersonating a psychiatrist. He sees that the Maniac has been arrested many times for impersonation and does not believe the Maniac's claim that he is mad and therefore not responsible for his actions. He seems intent on finding a way to make a charge against the Maniac stick. However, after enduring enough of the Maniac's double-talk, he becomes utterly exasperated and tells him to leave the station.

In act 2, Inspector Bertozzo returns as an important element in the play's closing farce. He knows that the Maniac is not the forensics expert that he is pretending to be and wants to expose him to the Superintendent and Sports Jacket. They forestall any revelation on the part of Bertozzo, as they believe that he is going to reveal the Maniac to be a judge, which would be disastrous, given that they have told the journalist that he is a forensics expert. Bertozzo must put up with a great number of kicks—every time he opens his mouth to protest the Maniac's deception, the Superintendent and Sports

Jacket must prevent him from doing so. These farcical kicks are more than just slapstick, however; they are designed to remind the audience of the physical abuses the anarchist endured during his interrogation. Like the other police officers, Bertozzo is wary of the journalist's questions, yet they, more so than he, are targets of her questioning.

Constable

The Constable is present in most of the play but has a fairly small role, speaking only occasionally. When ordered to do something by a superior, he follows orders immediately. However, he is not above a certain self-preserving caution, in that when he is questioned pointedly by the Maniac he is unwilling to commit himself by speaking plainly and also unwilling to show clear support of any superior whom the Maniac, as judge, appears to suspect of wrongdoing.

Maria Feletti

Known as the Journalist in Fo's play, the Feletti character arrives at the police station to ask questions about the growing scandal concerning the death of an anarchist suspect in police custody. At first, Sports Jacket wants to send her away, but the Maniac convinces him that he can use her to his benefit.

The Feletti character is a faithful representation of an experienced journalist: polite, cool, and hard-hitting in her questions. As Italians following the Pinelli case would have realized, this character is based on a real journalist, Camilla Cederna, who was then a reporter for the Italian weekly *L'espresso*. Cederna, like Feletti of *Accidental Death of an Anarchist*, uncovered real evidence of police corruption, not only with respect to the Pinelli case but also more broadly, in terms of Italian law enforcement and governmental establishments. Contrary to the Maniac, the Feletti character believes that scandal is beneficial, leading to real change and having the potential to deliver justice through the exposure of lawbreakers.

Maniac

The Maniac is the pivotal character in *Accidental Death of an Anarchist*. The part was acted by Fo himself in the original staging of the play. The character of the Maniac eclipses all other characters in every sense. He has by far the majority of lines, and he is by far the most interesting element of Fo's drama. Indeed, that it is difficult to distinguish between the police figures as personalities does not matter much, as the Maniac is the play's heart and soul. Onstage from the play's beginning to its end, the Maniac uses speech and actions to directly reflect the manipulations that the play is designed to expose.

At the beginning of *Accidental Death of an Anarchist*, the Maniac is in a Milan police station—the setting of the play—because he has been arrested for impersonating a psychiatrist. The inspector questioning him (Bertozzo) decides to let him go, however, because the Maniac's fast talking is just too much to bear. But the Maniac does not leave the police station; instead, he decides to continue with his impersonations. Specifically, he decides to impersonate a judge who is scheduled to arrive soon. In this guise, he questions several policemen and station officials about the death of a suspect, a case that has attracted much attention. In the course of his impersonation, the Maniac tricks the policemen and officials into revealing that they are part of a cover-up concerning the details of the suspect's death. (Before the play's end, the Maniac will impersonate two others, a forensics expert by the name of Captain Marcantonio Banzi Piccinni and a Vatican *chargé d'affaires* called Father Augusto Bernier.)

The Maniac is such a strong character in *Accidental Death of an Anarchist* because he embodies what he brings to light in his role as judge. First, as one who impersonates another, he reminds Fo's audiences that a common practice of the time was to send out police spies to infiltrate political groups. Second, as a character whose fast talking tricks the corrupt policemen, he is a trickster who gives them a dose of their own medicine. Even more specifically, the Maniac represents a dishonest interrogator, a policeman whose questioning amounts to coercion, entrapment, and abuse. Last, in the way that he consistently contradicts himself, he reminds audiences of the discrepant testimony of the police at the inquest and hearings that followed the real-life anarchist Giuseppe Pinelli's death. He is a reflection, in other words, of the distortion of facts for which the policemen involved in the actual case became known. For example, as quoted in Tom Behan's *Dario Fo*, a real-life Milan police officer is on record as speaking as follows at a hearing about whether or not he heard another officer say something when Pinelli was being interrogated:

> I'm not able to rectify or be precise about whether I heard that phrase because it was repeated, or because it was mentioned to me. As I believe I've already testified to having heard it, to having heard it directly; then, drawing things together, I don't believe that I heard it. However I'm not in a position to exclude that it may have been mentioned to me.

The Maniac is a manifestation of the madness surrounding him and all Italians during a time of corruption, unrest, and strife in Italian life. Still, as a farcical figure, he attests to Fo's belief that political theater with a serious intent need not be dry.

Sports Jacket

Sports Jacket is the policeman who, early in the play, calls Inspector Bertozzo's office and ends up having a conversation with the Maniac. In this conversation, the Maniac learns that a judge is being sent to ask questions about an anarchist suspect who died while being interrogated. Once he is impersonating the judge, the Maniac spends a great deal of time questioning Sports Jacket, with the result that the officer is exposed as being involved in an elaborate cover-up regarding the suspect.

Fo's audiences would have understood that Sports Jacket is a representation of a real officer involved in the real-life event on which the play is based. Specifically, Sports Jacket represents Luigi Calabresi, an officer who had been in the fourth-floor room of the Milan police station when the anarchist Giuseppe Pinelli plunged from the window. Calabresi sued a Milan publication for libel when the publication intimated that he had been wrongfully involved in the anarchist's death. Fo's costume for Sports Jacket refers to this trial, as Calabresi wore rolled-neck sweaters and sports jackets throughout. Calabresi also frequently rubbed his right hand during the trial, an action that many people believe indicated that this hand delivered the brutal blow to the back of Pinelli's neck. Fo's Sports Jacket delivers a punch to Inspector Bertozzo, and thereafter he often rubs the punching hand.

Because Sports Jacket believes that the Maniac is a judge who has been sent to investigate the death of the anarchist, he is by turns wary, nervous, belligerent, pleased, or relieved, depending on the nature of the Maniac's questions and moods. Apart from this, Sports Jacket tends to display brutal behavior, at least as far he can within the context of the play's amusing farce. Clearly, Fo wants to suggest that there was indeed a police officer at Milan headquarters who went too far in manhandling Pinelli, dealing the anarchist the terrible blow on the back of the neck that left the mark the pathologists found on his corpse.

Superintendent

The Superintendent of the play is much like Sports Jacket. He reacts defensively when the Maniac, as judge, poses questions that appear to suggest a suspicion of wrongdoing on his part; he is pleased when the Maniac seems to be supporting what he did when he interrogated the anarchist; he is nervous when he cannot quite figure out what the Maniac is up to in his questioning. As in the case of Sports Jacket, the Maniac succeeds in tricking the Superintendent into incriminating himself.

Reform versus Revolution

Those who wish to change society may think that instituting reforms is the way to go about it. Reformers have faith in existing structures and believe that these structures need only be perfected —or corrupt elements within them be rooted out— for desired changes to come about. Others who wish to change society for the better believe that what is called for is revolution, a radical restructuring of society and its institutions. Revolutionaries tend to think that reforms are mere bandages on never-healing sores, leading to temporary alleviation of a persistent problem, such as poverty, but never eliminating it. They believe, in short, that existing structures must be dismantled and that entirely new ones must take their place.

Fo's *Accidental Death of an Anarchist* is infused with revolutionary zeal, as is evident at the play's end, when the Maniac discourses on scandal. To the Maniac, scandals such as exposés of police corruption do little to bring about real change. Rather, scandal allows people to let off steam, with the result that the powers that be are in a stronger position than before. The implication is that scandal might lead to some reforms but never to true revolutionary change. In the following excerpt, the Maniac pretends to be translating the words of a pope who knew very well how scandal could be used to strengthen his position:

> MANIAC: Did you know that when Saint Gregory was elected Pope, he discovered that his subordinates were up to all kinds of skullduggery in an attempt to cover up various outrageous scandals? He was furious, and it was then that he uttered his famous phrase: *Nolimus aut velimus, omnibus gentibus, justitiam et veritatem.*

> JOURNALIST: I'm sorry, your Eminence ... I failed Latin three times....

> MANIAC: It means: 'Whether they want it or not, I shall impose truth and justice. I shall do what I can to make sure that these scandals explode in the most public way possible; and you need not fear that, in among the rot, the power of government will be undermined. Let the scandal come, because on the basis of that scandal a more durable power of the state will be founded!'

Topics for Further Study

- *Accidental Death of an Anarchist* employs many elements typical of farce. Research the characteristics of farce and write an essay on Fo's play as a farce.

- Research trickster literatures and write an essay comparing and contrasting figures from two different traditions, such as a Native American tradition and the African American Uncle Remus tradition.

- Research one of the American terrorist groups of the 1960s or 1970s, such as the Weather Underground or the Symbionese Liberation Army. What were their political beliefs and goals? Did they consider people acceptable terrorist targets? Who were the leaders of these organizations? What happened to them? Compile your findings into a report with appropriate subheadings.

- What were the political beliefs of anarchists such as Giuseppe Pinelli? Where did anarchist theories first develop? What are the basic tenets of anarchist politics? Present a report to your class that dispels misconceptions about anarchists and explains their core political ideals.

- At the time of writing *Accidental Death of an Anarchist*, Fo was running a drama group called La Comune. Research La Comune within the context of contemporary events in Italian social and political life. In an essay, explain how the group's ethos and goals are responses to what was happening in Italy at the time.

A bit later in the play, the Maniac speaks of scandal again:

MANIAC: They've never tried to hush up these scandals. And they're right not to. That way, people can let off steam, get angry, shudder at the thought of it … 'Who do these politicians think they are?' 'Scumbag generals!' 'Murderers!' And they get more and more angry, and then, burp! A little liberatory burp to relieve their social indigestion.

Fear and Submission

During periods of social unrest or general crisis, the political scene in a nation becomes tense. Different groups believe they have the answer to the nation's ills or a way to deal with the crisis and threat, and each group attempts to wrest control from those in power. The coalition in power naturally wishes to retain control and will often go to great lengths to do so. During the time period in which Fo wrote *Accidental Death of an Anarchist*, Italy was undergoing just such a period of extreme social unrest, when those in power wondered if they would be able to maintain authority and control.

Particularly disturbing to the authorities was the growing influence of certain groups whose politics were "far" left, calling for a radical restructuring of society, not simply reform. In an effort to discredit such groups in the eyes of the general public, members of the Italian police force —some say with the support of the government— began sanctioning the activities of agents posing as far leftists and committing terrorist acts in their name. Bomb after bomb exploded in Italian cities, and the general public began to believe that order was escaping them. This fear on the part of the general public was precisely what was sought, as a fearful and uncertain public is a public unlikely to commit to major change at the governmental level for fear of yet more chaos. Fomenting chaos and encouraging fear are standard tactics of the corrupt and manipulative. Entirely dishonest, this is nevertheless a sure way to influence voters' behavior.

At many points in the play, in which information is cited from actual documents, Fo's characters convey these various ideas. In the following excerpt, for example, the Maniac speaks of a plot to discredit "the Left":

> MANIAC: At the start you served a useful function: something had to be done to stop all the strikes ... So they decided to start a witch-hunt against the Left. But now things have gone a bit too far.

In the following excerpt, somewhat later in the play, Fo's fictional journalist cites actual facts concerning the makeup of the activist group to which the (real) anarchist belonged. Of the ten members of the group, four were infiltrators, as the Journalist points out:

> JOURNALIST: OK. So let's take a look behind that façade. What do we find? Out of the ten members of the [anarchist's] group, two of them were your own people, two informers, or rather, spies and provocateurs. One

was a Rome fascist, well-known to everyone except the aforementioned pathetic group of anarchists, and the other was one of your own officers, disguised as an anarchist.

The Journalist speaks again along similar lines still later in the play:

> JOURNALIST: *(Taking some papers from a folder)* ... And I suppose nobody's told you either that out of a total of 173 bomb attacks that have happened in the past year and a bit, at a rate of twelve a month, one every three days—out of 173 attacks, as I was saying *(She reads from a report)* at least 102 have been proved to have been organised by fascist [rightist] organisations, aided or abetted by the police, with the explicit intention of putting the blame on Left-wing political groups.

The Trickster

The Maniac is a variant of a trickster figure, a character who acts mad or simple but who is actually invested with more sense than anybody around him. Tricksters fool those who are vain or who believe themselves cleverer than everybody else. Tricksters are quite often lesser societal figures tricked by those more elevated. They belong to the ranks of the common people, appearing in stories as an assertion of their worthiness in the face of an elite group's disdain and ignorance. Every nation has literary traditions employing trickster figures. One very well-known trickster series in the American literary canon uses animals as characters (as do so many trickster traditions). This series is Joel Chandler Harris's Uncle Remus stories of Brer Rabbit and Brer Fox. Harris compiled these stories from those of African American storytellers, building on original African traditions. In the American context, these African American stories of seemingly weak characters winning out over stronger figures reveal the slave's or newly freed slave's assertion of his own wisdom against an elite that usually refused to see it.

Fo employs the trickster Maniac in *Accidental Death of an Anarchist* most probably in order to foster a sense of empowerment in his audiences.

After all, the play addresses an event pointing to covert police criminality and likely governmental support of such wrongdoing. To know that one is being fooled by one's leaders or to believe that they are corrupt is to feel helpless, powerless, confused. Why vote if one is voting for crooks? If one's leaders are dishonest, why should anyone be honest? The clever trickster figure in Fo's play effectively exposes the lies and collusions of the corrupt police officers, conveying a sense that the truth can indeed be known and justice can indeed be served.

The Bawdy and Slapstick

Fo's employment of bawdy humor and slapstick action is, like his use of the trickster Maniac, a populist component of his play—an element designed to appeal to all audiences and not simply to elite ones. Bawdy humor focuses on bodily functions, such as the fun Fo derives from the lustily farting Maniac: "Yes, you can tell him that too: Anghiari and Bertozzo couldn't give a [sh—t]! *(He lets out a tremendous raspberry [fart])* Prrruttt. Yes, it was Bertozzo who did the raspberry. Alright, no need to get hysterical …!" Slapstick humor is similarly body oriented, as it involves characters tripping or falling—somehow being made ridiculous (without any lasting harm coming to them). An example of slapstick in *Accidental Death of an Anarchist* is when Bertozzo receives a big punch in the face from the inspector, who believes Bertozzo has sent the raspberry his way.

Bawdy and slapstick humor is considered populist because it is humor that anyone can appreciate—such as a derisive fart.

Alienation Effects

Playwrights with strong political convictions such as Fo tend to employ and develop dramatic techniques that distance the audience from the work. These techniques might be called alienation effects, after the language of the playwright who pioneered many distancing methods, the German Bertolt Brecht. Brecht thought it important to alienate the audience from the play being performed so that they would think critically about what they were watching. For example, he would present characters performing more or less typical, everyday actions in his plays, but he would make sure that the acting was just stilted enough so that the audience would see these actions in a new light. What is strange about things so many of us do? he wanted his audiences to ask. What if things were done differently? How might the world change for the better? Two of Brecht's most famous plays are *Mother Courage and Her Children* and *The Good Woman of Setzuan.*

Other distancing effects besides acting techniques that are not quite realistic are, for example, self-reflexive strategies. This means that a playwright includes moments when the play refers to itself as a play. For example, the actors might refer to themselves as actors, or the actors might speak directly to the audience, destroying the illusion of "reality on stage" and reminding the audience that a play, something made up, is taking place. Moments such as these disturb the audience's identification with the actors and story, encouraging viewers to evaluate what is transpiring. Here is a self-reflexive moment from *Accidental Death of an Anarchist*:

> JOURNALIST: And I suppose you have plenty more of these very well-trained operatives scattered around the Left groups?

> SUPERINTENDENT: I see no reason to deny it, Miss. Yes we do.

> JOURNALIST: I think you're just calling my bluff, there, Superintendent!

> SUPERINTENDENT: Not at all … In fact you may be interested to know that we have one or two right here in the audience tonight, as usual … Watch this.

> *He claps his hands. We hear a number of voices from different parts of the auditorium.*

> VOICES: Sir …? Yessir …! Sir …!

> *The* MANIAC *laughs, and turns to the audience.*

> MANIAC: Don't worry—they're all actors. The real ones sit tight and

don't say a word.

As this excerpt demonstrates, Fo has his actors speak directly about and to the audience.

Social Unrest and the "Hot Autumn" of 1969 in Italy

Politicians who were voted into Italy's parliament in the 1960s and 1970s had much to answer for. Italy's working class was fed up—with dangerous working conditions, long hours, low pay, expensive and uninhabitable housing, poor benefit packages, and more. Mobilizing, the working classes began to march and strike. Left-wing organizations, furthermore, were flourishing and gaining power, including those on the Far Left, favoring revolution over reform. The autumn of 1969 in Italy is known as the "Hot Autumn" of working class and student protest, as unrest had reached a height. On October 15, fifty thousand workers demonstrated in Milan, and on November 28, one hundred thousand engineers demonstrated in Rome. Other disturbances and changes were afoot as well. This was the time, for example, of feminist agitation, so that in November a law legalizing divorce in Italy was passed.

Contributing to the political and social heat of the time was the fact that, as in the United States and elsewhere, radical political organizations on both the left and the right of the political spectrum were turning to terrorism. As the Communist-inclined Weather Underground was blowing up buildings in the United States, similar underground organizations were doing the same in Italy. Indeed, as the Journalist says in *Accidental Death of an Anarchist*, 173 bomb attacks occurred in Italy in the space of little more than a year during this time. The anarchist who died at Milan police headquarters and whose death is the subject of Fo's play had been arrested on suspicion of carrying out a Hot Autumn bombing at the National Agricultural Bank in Piazza Fontana in Milan on November 12, 1969.

Compare & Contrast

- **Late 1960s to early 1970s:** Italians are mobilized by radical political philosophies calling for drastic changes to cure such ills as low wages and poor working conditions in factories.

  Today: Italian workers wonder whether the considerable gains won following the protests of the 1960s are threatened by the developments of a globalizing world economy. They worry that greater competition among nations will lead companies to cut worker salaries and benefits in order to remain competitive.

- **Late 1960s to early 1970s:** Countercultural youths, like the hippies, protest against what they perceive as repressive elements within Italian life, such as the premium placed on sexual abstinence before marriage. Italian feminists also stage protests.

Today: While the most extreme positions held by counterculture enthusiasts are rejected, Italian society is radically different. For example, women are now integral in the professional workforce, and contraception is widely practiced.

- **Late 1960s to early 1970s:** The Roman Catholic Church begins losing some of its power within Italy, as is seen in the Italian government's legalization of divorce in 1969.

  Today: While most Italians identify themselves as Roman Catholics and thousands of mourners poured into the streets following the death of Pope John Paul II (1920–2005), less than half the population attends church regularly.

- **Late 1960s to early 1970s:** The business tycoon Silvio Berlusconi builds a massive complex of apartments just outside Milan, called Milano 2. Some say that he won this project with secret help and backing from a powerful anti-Communist organization known as Propaganda

2.

Today: Berlusconi, elected twice as Italy's prime minister, is subject to charges of bribery, and a new term, *Berlusconismo*, begins circulating in Italy. The term refers to a way of life in which an Italian lives in a house built by Berlusconi, shops at markets owned by Berlusconi, eats at restaurants owned by Berlusconi, watches television stations controlled by Berlusconi, and so on.

Giuseppe Pinelli and Pietro Valpreda

Giuseppe Pinelli and Pietro Valpreda were two anarchists arrested in the aftermath of the Hot Autumn Piazza Fontana bombing of November 12, 1969. Pinelli, a forty-one-year-old railway worker, was married with two daughters. Valpreda was a ballet dancer. Within seventy-two hours of his arrest, Pinelli was dead under suspicious circumstances. According to police statements, he had thrown himself from a window while being interrogated. However, there were discrepancies in the policemen's stories and in the evidence. At an inquest, suicide was not concluded; the death was deemed an accident. Neither Pinelli (posthumously) nor Valpreda was ever convicted of the bombing, nor were any other suspected persons, all of whom were members of neofascist organizations. Working against those trying to convict Pinelli was the sense that he was not the type of activist to carry out such an attack. This idea, that the bombing was carried out not by amateurs but by paramilitary agents, is expressed in *Accidental Death of an Anarchist*, when the Journalist characterizes the group to which the anarchist of Fo's play belongs:

> JOURNALIST: So what did you do? Even though you were well aware that to construct—let alone plant—a bomb of such complexity, would take the skills and experience of professionals—probably military people—you decided to go chasing after this fairly pathetic group of anarchists and completely dropped all other lines of inquiry among certain parties who shall remain nameless but you know who I mean.

A plaque dedicated to Pinelli can still be seen in Piazza Fontana, as most Italians believe he was a victim of police brutality.

Critical Overview

Fo was already a major cultural figure in Italy when *Accidental Death of an Anarchist* was staged. Indeed, his credibility and influence were such that he was provided with copies of actual inquest and police documents as he was composing his play. *Accidental Death of an Anarchist* opened approximately one year after Giuseppe Pinelli's death, in December 1970, and it was a major hit all over Italy as it toured and played to thousands. Italian support of the play suggests the degree to which Italians were critical of authorities at the time.

Although another of Fo's plays, *Mistero buffo*, is considered his most popular in Italy, *Accidental Death of an Anarchist* is said to be his second most popular. Outside Italy, it is Fo's most-performed play, partly owing to its searing indictment of police corruption and strong suggestion that a similarly corrupt government body is underwriting this corruption. As Tom Behan indicates in *Dario Fo: Revolutionary Theatre*, directors around the world who want to respond to corruption in their own midst have turned to *Accidental Death of an Anarchist* to galvanize their audiences to political action, despite the great risks involved in doing so:

> Fo claims that *Accidental Death of an Anarchist* has been the most performed play in the world over the

last 40 years. Its pedigree certainly is impressive: productions in at least 41 countries in very testing circumstances: fascist Chile, Ceausescu's Romania and apartheid South Africa. In Argentina and Greece the cast of early productions were all arrested.

Because Fo allows changes to be made to his script, foreign directors can include material that makes the play relevant to their particular local situation. Of course, if *Accidental Death of an Anarchist* were not as well written and entertaining as it is, it would not be such a favorite choice of the world's directors and drama groups. What has made Fo's and this play's reputation, finally, is his great skill as a dramatist and theatrical innovator. However, many of Fo's innovations are, paradoxically, adaptations from past theatrical traditions. Joseph Farrell discusses this paradox in "Dario Fo: *Zanni* and *Giullare*," from the essay collection *The Commedia Dell'Arte: From the Renaissance to Dario Fo*:

> The affection for, and identification with, figures from Italian theatrical tradition, be it *Arlecchino* [Harlequin] or the *giullare* [a performer who would travel from village to village], are perfect illustrations of one of the most striking and paradoxical features of the work of Dario Fo—his relentless

search for models from the past with whom he can identify. If on the one hand Fo is customarily seen, and indeed goes out of his way to present himself, as the subversive, the iconoclastic revolutionary,… at the same time his theatrical style is based not on any avant-garde, but on the approaches and techniques practiced by performers of centuries past.

As Farrell writes, the "figure of the *giullare*," which "provides Fo with a focus and a model" for much of his work, "is a quintessentially medieval figure, who flourished approximately from the Tenth to the Fifteenth centuries, in other words in the period before the blossoming of *Commedia dell'arte*." Still, the tradition of the *commedia dell'arte*—from which the figure of the Harlequin derives—is also an important source of inspiration for Fo. Troupes of professional actors made up the *commedia* groups. They would perform for common people in village squares as soon as they would for aristocrats on polished stages, improvising dialogue within the set limits of stock plots.

In the essay collection *Studies in the Commedia Dell'Arte*, Christopher Cairns explores Fo's relationship to *commedia* tradition in his essay "Dario Fo and the *Commedia Dell'Arte*." He points out that Fo's interest in this tradition's figures and techniques developed only after he had immersed himself in the tradition of the *giullare* for many years. Fo's new-found interest, however, resulted in the curious discovery that he had been implementing *commedia* techniques all along:

> In London in 1988, Fo admitted that he had come late to the formal study of the *commedia dell'arte*, but had found with some surprise that he had been involved in similar theatrical practice (with different roots, in variety, the circus, the silent film) already for many years.

In a comment on the *commedia* aspects of Fo's play *Harlequin* (1985), Cairns describes the relationship between tradition and innovation so characteristic of Fo's work in general:

> The extraordinary vogue for the *commedia dell'arte* as a performance language in the contemporary theatre has given rise to two distinct conventions. First [there is] the 'archaeological' reconstruction of the working methods, costumes, masks and relationships between the well-known stereotype characters, refined and polished to a high degree of professional performance.... Secondly, we have the adaptation or 'selection' of styles from past traditions of *commedia* for modern uses: a bringing face to face with contemporary social and political

causes of a deep-rooted European theatrical tradition, particularly since the 1960s. It is to this second *modern* convention that Dario Fo's *Harlequin* belongs.

Thus, many critics do not hesitate to argue that there are *commedia* elements in those of Fo's plays written even before his formal study of the tradition.

What Do I Read Next?

- Fo's most popular play is *Mistero buffo*, which means "The Comedic Mystery." It features the comedic antics of a jester in the medieval tradition of the "jongleurs," traveling entertainers whose performances flouted the authority of church and state. It has been seen by millions of Italians and shows Fo's grounding in popular storytelling traditions. This one-man show satirizing landowners, the Roman Catholic Church, and the Italian government was first performed by Fo in 1969.

- The *Complete Plays of Vladimir Mayakovsky*, translated by Guy Daniels, contains Mayakovsky's *Mystery-Bouffe* (1918), an inspiration for Fo's own *Mistero buffo*. Mayakovsky, a Russian writer who engaged in subversive socialist political activities, was one of Fo's many influences, thanks to his revolutionary zeal on the part of Russia's then-disenfranchised peasants and lower classes.

- The *Uncle Remus* tales first published by Joel Chandler Harris in book form in 1880 were told to him by African American storytellers. These are tales employing trickster figures like the Maniac.

- The four plays of *Female Parts: One Woman Plays* (1981) were written by Fo in collaboration with his longtime partner, Franca Rame. Rame acted in these plays when they were first produced.

Sources

Behan, Tom, *Dario Fo: Revolutionary Theatre*, Pluto Press, 2000, p. 67.

Cairns, Christopher, "Dario Fo and the *Commedia Dell'-Arte*," in *Studies in the Commedia Dell'Arte*, edited by David J. George and Christopher J. Gossip, University of Wales Press, 1993, p. 1.

Farrell, Joseph, "Dario Fo: *Zanni* and *Giullare*," in *The Commedia Dell'Arte: From the Renaissance to Dario Fo*, edited by Christopher Cairns, Edwin Mellon Press, 1989, pp. 1-2.

Fo, Dario, *Accidental Death of an Anarchist*, translated by Ed Emery, in *Dario Fo: Plays 1*, Methuen, 1992, pp. 127, 136, 137, 152, 176, 190, 191, 193, 198, 200, 202.

Further Reading

Brecht, Bertolt, *Brecht on Theatre: The Development of an Aesthetic*, edited and translated by John Willett, Eyre Methuen, 1964.

> Willett's compilation of Brecht's writings on theater is a thorough introduction to the dramatist's evolving concerns in his influential career as a writer and director of political theater.

Cardullo, Bert, and Robert Knopf, eds., *Theater of the Avant-Garde, 1890–1950: A Critical Anthology*, Yale University Press, 2001.

> This anthology assembles the statements, manifestoes, and opinions of major drama theorists and practitioners, some of whom, like Bertolt Brecht, influenced Fo.

Hirst, David L., *Dario Fo and Franca Rame*, St. Martin's Press, 1989.

> Hirst's book is a comprehensive general introduction to the works and collaboration of Dario Fo and Franca Rame.

Mitchell, Tony, *Dario Fo: People's Court Jester*, Methuen, 1986.

> A well-known Fo scholar, Mitchell

provides insight into how Fo's political convictions inform his works. Photographs that capture the farcical and daring nature of Fo's theater are included.

—————————, ed. *File on Fo*, Methuen Drama, 1989.

Mitchell has compiled excerpts from writings by critics on Fo and Rame and by Fo and Rame themselves. Mitchell's choice of excerpts is useful and fair, as he includes evaluations both critical and admiring.